# The Roadmap:
## A Simple Guide to Understanding the Bible

By

Craig Dockstader

And

Matt Simonis

Copyright © 2017 by Craig Dockstader and Matt Simonis

All rights reserved.

ISBN: 1532707339
ISBN-13: 978-1532707339

# DEDICATIONS

Craig Dockstader:

For my girls: Lisa, Zoe, and Kady

Matt Simonis:

For Willie

# TABLE OF CONTENTS

Welcome .................................................................................. 1
Communicating with God ...................................................... 2
Memorizing Verses ................................................................. 6
How the Bible was Formed ..................................................... 8
What is God Like? ................................................................. 13
Who is Jesus? ........................................................................ 16
It or He? The Holy Spirit ....................................................... 20
Salvation ............................................................................... 24
Faith ..................................................................................... 29
Life's Struggles ..................................................................... 33
The Church ........................................................................... 37
Spiritual Gifts ....................................................................... 41
Living for God ...................................................................... 46
Blessed Hope ........................................................................ 49
Millennial Reign ................................................................... 55
Final Judgement ................................................................... 59
New Heaven and a New Earth .............................................. 62
Now What? ........................................................................... 64
Appendix A: Glossary ........................................................... 66
Appendix B: Suggested Memory Verses ............................... 68

# ACKNOWLEDGMENTS

Craig Dockstader:

Thank you to Jesus for giving me the vision to see a need, the talent to write and a passion to meet the needs of others. My girls: Lisa, Zoe and Kady for being my support as I fulfill God's call on my life. You're awesome!

Matt Simonis

Jesus and my wife. Without them, I'm not much.

From the both of us:

Special thanks to our team that helped make this happen: Brad Hudec, David LeMasters, Angie Rich, Bobbi Brossard, Stephen Masters, Lisa Dockstader, and Dewan Simonis.

# WELCOME

Welcome to The Roadmap!

The route of our learning about God is commonly called a path. The Bible uses this analogy several times. Our goal is for this guide to help you navigate your way on this path.

The Bible is the light for our walk on this path. This study is NOT anything new. It just highlights some specifics of the Bible to speed things up a bit, especially if you've never dug to find out what the Bible says and teaches.

Whether you are simply interested in learning about the Bible, already have crossed the line of faith, or even if you are a seasoned church 'pro', this workbook is designed to meet you wherever you are in your journey.

Over the next few pages, you will traverse through a variety of topics ranging from how the Bible was formed… to core beliefs that students learn in Bible school. You'll find this journey to be a step-by-step path that leads you to a fuller understanding of all the things we have in Christ Jesus.

There are times when the topic needs to be explained so we might seem a little wordy, but most of the time you will have a chance to discover the details yourself by looking it up in the Bible.

You can even find a Glossary of common church words (found at the back).

You will read scripture, learn verses, and gain personal perspective on what you believe and why you believe it. Our hope is that you will not only gain a foundation, but ultimately a map that will lead you to your ultimate destination… a deeper relationship with Jesus Christ.

The Roadmap is just that, a tool to help you stay on the right path. God's word is the lamp, guiding our steps (Psalm 119:105). There are lots of tools out there. This is just one of them.

So, if you're ready, buckle up and let the journey begin!

# COMMUNICATING WITH GOD

Society has taught us that, in order to get to heaven, we need to act a certain way, say certain things, be a good person… and the list goes on and on. But that just isn't true.

God created us to have relationship with Him. "For we are his workmanship, created in Christ Jesus for good works, which God prepared beforehand, that we should walk in them." (Ephesians 2:10 NIV)

Every great relationship has two important aspects. One, dedication to the other involved in the relationship, and two, continuous work to improve the relationship. For example, if you look at any successful marriage, you will see these two simple aspects in action on a regular basis.

Every relationship has ups and downs, as well as moments where one may feel unworthy or unwanted. We have all felt this way at times, even when it comes to our relationship with Jesus.

We are also encouraged to not be anxious about anything but to present our requests to God through prayer.
1. Look up Philippians 4:6-7.
    a. List all the things we should be anxious about in this space: __

Prayer is just talking to God. He hears us if we pray out loud, or if we pray silently.

Prayer is a very important part of developing a relationship with God. There are all kinds of views on how to pray. Many of these views are coming from sources outside of the Bible. This is just one example of The Roadmap existing to help you develop that relationship with God by understanding more about Him, plus using the Bible as our 'manual'.

Our relationship with God is not based on a checklist of doing good things and avoiding bad things, nor based on fear of failure. It's about His dedication and continuous work to be closer to us. Being a good person or doing the right things cannot help you get to heaven. The fact remains… it all comes down to Jesus.
2. Read John 14:6.
    a. How many ways are there to the Father? _____

Of course, the next question is how do we have a relationship with God and get to be with Him in heaven.
3. The answer can be found in Ephesians 2:8-9. Check it out.
    a. Salvation (being saved) is not achieved by what we _____.

Much like our relationship with a physical person depends on communication (listening and talking), our relationship with God is based on our communication with Him through prayer. Prayer is how we share our needs, our concerns, and the desires of our heart.

So many of us have said, "Why Pray? Does it really matter if I pray? Does God really hear me? Does God answer me when I pray?" These are questions we have all asked, and perhaps you have a vague answer.

What does Jesus say about prayer?

4. Look up John 10:27.
    a. For those who _____, He knows them and they _____ Him.
What about the Apostle Paul, what did he say?
5. Find Romans 10:13.
    a. What happens when we call out to Him? "For whosoever shall call upon the name of the Lord shall be saved."

Again, our relationship with God is based on prayer AND listening (communication is two-way), just like any other relationship.

Let's consider a few more questions about prayer:
6. Read James 4:1-3.
    a. Give two reasons why God may not give us what we ask of Him: ① We try and take without asking. ② Your asking for the wrong reasons. Ask God for wisdom to find the right path
7. Take a look at 1 John 1:9. (1John, 2 John, and 3 John, are small books found right before the book of Revelation, near the back of your Bible. Don't confuse these with the Book of John, one of the accounts of the life and ministry of Jesus on earth.) instead of asking for $$.
    a. One of our topics when we pray to God is to: Confess + ask for forgiveness of our sins.
8. Now look at Isaiah 59:2.
    a. What has separated us from God? Our iniquities.
9. Look up Psalm 66:16-20.
    a. If we don't confess, what happens? The Lord will not listen.
10. Read Luke 18:9-14.
    a. How does your attitude affect your prayers?
    _____
    _____

11. Find John 16:24.
    a. When we have the right attitude, what can we freely do in our prayers?
    _____

12. Consider Hebrews 4:16.
    a. When we have the right attitude, how can we approach God?
    _____

13. Read 1 John 5:14-15.
    a. How can we be certain God will answer our prayers?
    _____

14. Look up Romans 8:26-27.
    a. To intercede is to 'ask on someone's behalf.' Because we are _____ what does the Holy Spirit do on our behalf? _____

15. One of the most famous sermons in the Bible is found in Matthew 5-7. Read the verses from chapter 7:7-12. What three things are we to do? _____, _____, and _____.

16. Look up John 16:23 and put your finger there. Then check out 1 Timothy 2:5. Compare these verses.
    a. If we pray for the will of God, in Jesus' name, what happens?
    _____
    _____

3

17. Read John 15:7.
    a. How can you remain in Him?
    _____
    _____

18. Find 1 Thessalonians 5:17.
    a. When is it a good time to pray? _____

You may have heard others pray out loud, and at the end of their prayer they say something like, "...In Jesus' name we pray, Amen." This comes from John 14:13. Go ahead and look up that verse. Additionally, the word "amen" means 'let it be so'. The combination of the two make a nice close to a prayer, but they are not required for God to hear you.

Prayer time with God is intended to be personal and fulfilling. He is our Father and we should be able to go right to our Father without hesitation. For those reading this that have not had a great Father figure in their lives, this can be a challenge. It comes down to trust.

Remember that communication is two-way. God can 'speak' to us in many ways. We can receive instruction from the Bible, we can receive godly advice/input from a trusted source, or a myriad of ways. A classic example of another way is noted in a great story found in 1 Kings 18:20-40, God can use a 'still small voice'.

Journaling is a great way to take all your thoughts and prayers, collectively, and lay them out on the table before God. This is a deeply personal thing you can do. Through journaling, you can see what prayers have been answered, life-changes made in both yourself and those you prayed for, and then see how God is answering. The journal, in a way, is a record of your quest. Since we are using the 'path' analogy, think of it as a scrapbook you've put together along the way. You can see mountains passed, rivers crossed, and prayers being answered.

We can be completely open and honest with God. God never hurts us, only the enemy of our souls (the devil) does that. It is OK to treat God just like a regular father. If you're happy, you may want to write out why. If you're sad, let it flow from you to release the burden. If you're mad, let it out. God can take it! Write out whatever you want. For many, they write out what God is doing. And for most, they write out certain prayers – usually the deep/intense ones.

Additional: In our technology driven world, you can journal by writing in a notebook or use your mobile device or computer. OneNote (a common Microsoft app) is a great application for journaling. But whatever method you pick, use it. A journey doesn't exist if it is just memories in your head. Think of journaling as taking pictures along your journey on the path of life. You may be feeling down and alone one day and you decide to refer back… where you find God loving you through life's tough route.

'Communicating With God' Answer Key:
- (Personal, but God's wants our list to be blank)
- One
- Do
- Listen
- Follow
- We are saved
- You are asking with wrong motives, or not having a loving heart, or the like
- Confess our sins
- We have been separated from God
- The Lord will not listen
- (Personal)
- Ask for anything
- With confidence
- When we are asking for His will, not our own
- Sinners
- Intercedes for us
- Ask
- Seek
- Knock
- God, our Father, will give what we ask for
- His word needs to remain in us
- All the time

# MEMORIZING VERSES

An important step in the process of learning more about God is to memorize verses from the Bible. There are many reasons why you would do this, but Psalm 119:11 offers one of the best reasons. It says, "I have hidden your word in my heart that I might not sin against you." (NIV).

Memorizing verses helps you. This should become part of your normal routine in your daily 'walk' with God. You will be surprised how often you will remember a verse at the very moment you need it.

For many, memorizing can be a challenge. They don't think they have the mental skills to actually remember. And, just because someone knows the Bible, they may not be using it right (living what it says). This may seem a little strange to say, but this may actually be true.

Memorizing Bible verses is much like working out (our brains). When you start, it seems like lots of work to achieve just a little. But then it gets easier, much easier, once you've succeeded just a little. In other words, you may find it takes a lot of work to memorize a small handful of verses; but suddenly, you realize it doesn't take nearly as long, to commit a verse (or even several verses) to memory.

For many, they just read the verse over and over (and over) until they have it in their short-term memory. Then they can stretch it (move it) to long-term memory by refreshing a few times a day to see if they can recall it. For some, they find greater success by writing it down repeatedly until it sinks in. This is a great way to learn more than one verse at a time, as we begin to visually 'see' the words in our head.

Here is a helpful tool when it comes to memorizing: Have a Bible on one side of the room and the blank paper on the other side. With the verse selected and the Bible open to it, read just the first sentence (or phrase) and then walk across the room and write it down. Repeat this until the whole sentence can be written without having to walk back across the room. Once the first sentence is known, then begin adding the next sentence, all the while, writing down BOTH sentences each time, cementing the first sentence while you work on the second.

Then, as you add the third sentence, if applicable, you are reinforcing the first and second sentence (or phrase). When you can walk across the room and do it all in one effort, it is in your short-term memory. Then, by repeating your success just a few times a day, the verse makes its way to your long-term.

We have a list of Great Memory Verses found at the end of this book. But here are a few that are usually memorized first:
- John 3:16
- Ephesians 2:8-9
- Romans 3:23, 6:23, 5:8, 10:9-10 (these from Romans are commonly called "the Roman Road" (to salvation)).

We should mention that it is a great idea to memorize the books of the Bible. Start with the New

Testament (NT) ones first. Then the Old Testament (OT). If the OT list is too hard, don't fret. Knowing the NT books is VERY helpful when it comes to finding them quickly (while you look up verses).

Note: There are additional memory 'tools' that can be used to memorize lists. For example, come up with a sentence that uses the first letter from your list. The sentence doesn't even have to make sense; it just helps you remember the list. Also, using the writing trick above is very helpful for memorizing the books of the Bible.

# HOW THE BIBLE WAS FORMED

The Bible is made up of the Old Testament (39 'books') and the New Testament (27 'books'); for a total of 66. The Old Testament begins with creation and stops before the time of Jesus. The New Testament is from the time just before Jesus to the end of the time when the Apostles were traveling and ministering.

The specifics aren't exactly known, but the writing of all 66 books spanned over approximately 1500 years by about 40 different authors. There are translations in countless languages. But the Old Testament (we will refer to this as the 'OT') was written originally in Hebrew and Aramaic. The New Testament (the 'NT') was originally penned in Greek.

The history of how the Bible came to be (into our modern day single collection) is a little complicated. Most books were written as the events happened, or recalled through 'oral reciting' (a common practice to document history through memorizing the content) until they could be written down. Either way, eventually these books were penned into a format that has lasted for centuries.

All of the books were written down (in some manner) before the printing press, so only hand copies were available. But painful care was taken to make exact copies. For example, for making copies of portions of the OT, the transcriber (the person doing the copying) would ink a copy, by hand, letter by letter. After writing a passage, they would count all the words in the original and the copy – this number must match or the copy was destroyed. Then, they would count half way in to find the center word on both – it had to be the same word or the copy was destroyed. They repeated the process by counting just the single letters – total and the letter half way. If there was a discrepancy, the copy was destroyed. This practice preserved the copy accuracy for hundreds of years.

The formation of our collection of 66 books began to take shape shortly after the time of the Apostles came to an end. Within about 400 to 500 years, most of the collection was agreed upon. There were lots of scrolls and other written documents considered, but we ended up with just 66. The criteria were simple, based on these 5 questions:[1]

- Was the book written by a prophet of God?
    - There is common historical knowledge as to who the 'real' prophets were. Writings from others were not considered. This is the primary factor and eliminated a majority of the possible options.
- Was the writer authenticated by miracles to confirm his message?
    - Related to the first question, did this particular prophet have a life that confirmed their message?
- Does the book tell the truth about God, with no falsehood or contradiction?
    - This eliminated several more that contradicted accepted books from questions one and two.
- Does the book invoke a divine capacity to transform lives?
    - This goes beyond just encouragement, but to really have an impact on lives, proving God's inspiration.

---

[1] (GotQuestions, 2002)

- Was the book accepted as God's Word by the people to whom it was first delivered?
    - Much like question four... an immediate acceptance would have an impact, and thus become common knowledge.

You may have heard people speak of letters or books that are not in the Bible. If the previous conditions were not met, they were not considered 'canon' and not placed within the sixty-six books of the Bible.

When it came to translating the collection of 66 books into other languages, the task became much harder. Different languages have different 'syntaxes'. For example, in English we might say, "The red ball." But for most other languages, they say, "The ball red." If one translates word-for-word (called trans-literal translation), then the 'true' meaning (referred to as 'translating for content') could be in question.

There is a risk of personal preference[2], then, when it comes to translating for content. And many translations reveal this. So, the more scholarly translations, the ones you use for intense study, are the ones translated by large teams with a variety of church backgrounds.

For scholarly study, it is best to study a version that is as accurate as possible 'to the original meaning' of the texts. For many, though, readability is important. Choosing comes down to personal preference. For most Christ-followers, a version that is both readable and accurate is a good choice.

As you work through this section, our hope is that you will gain clarity and examine what the Bible says on your own through the scripture provided.
1. Look up 2 Timothy 3:16.
    a. What are the scriptures useful for?
    _____
    _____
2. Find 1 Thessalonians 2:13.
    a. What does the Bible say when we accept the word of God as a word from Him and not from just another person? _____
3. Flip back to 2 Peter 1:20-21.
    a. How do we know who the author was?
    _____

In some cases, the author identifies himself, like Paul, when he wrote letters to the church at Thessalonica (1 & 2 Thessalonians). Paul starts with a greeting and why he is writing, proceeds with the content of the letter, and then closing comments or a prayer.

---

[2] As you may have learned already, many churches have differing beliefs. For most evangelical churches (those that teach salvation is through Jesus – more details on that later), the salvation message is the same and most of the differences beyond that are minor. But in the area of translation, there is a risk that a person may select a word choice that may be 'more fitting' with their (differing beliefs).

There are cases, we are not certain who the author was. Over the course of a thousand years, about forty different writers authored what we have as our Bible. Many of these authors never knew each other, yet the constant theme and message remained: God and his consistent love for us.

Each book of the Bible falls within a specific style of writing and message for the reader. These styles range from historical narrative, prophecy (including end-time events), proverbial sayings, legal issues, poetry, songs, and genealogy.

Many parts of the Old Testament have been validated by archaeological discoveries like the Dead Sea Scrolls. Once an older copy is found, it is checked to see if there are any additions, deletions, or changes. The Dead Sea Scrolls pre-dated many copies by about 600 years with very few and minor differences, proving the integrity and accuracy of the copying process.

Most NT books were simply letters that were read in synagogues (a church building for the Jews), churches, and towns – passed around from church to church to have the greatest impact.

Additional: Most NT churches met in private homes. Even some prominent church buildings were small. For example, the church building at Ephesus was only approximately 15' x 40'. This gives us a great model to follow, in that, nearly all church 'ministry' did not happen at a church building.

And when it comes to the New Testament, there is substantial evidence supporting the gospel accounts. There are four different accounts of the life of Jesus on earth, written by four different men to four different audiences. These are called the 'gospels' (from the Greek word meaning 'good news').

Think of it this way; you and I see a car accident. We both see the start, the middle and the end. However, you may see something in your view I was unable to see, adding depth to the story when we tell it to those investigating the accident. The same is true with the gospels. Not every detail will be the same in each account, yet the content is there. There may be slight differences of perspective, but the truth remains.

Although there are thoughts or debates that one scripture may seem to be or say something different than the others, the truth, themes, languages and culture of the time are all the same.

So why translate into the common language? Well, most languages change over time. English is spoken all over the world, but there are many accents and figures of speech that are not common in all areas. 'Modern' translations permit the readers of that period to read the Bible in their own language. The best example of this is the King James Version. When this was written, this was the common language of the day. Nowadays, it is rather difficult to read.

Which version of the Bible is the best? Well, it depends what you want to do with your reading. Here are just a FEW examples of typical English versions:
- For scholarly work, the King James Version (KJV) (written in old English) and the New International Version (NIV) (very good at concepts) have the most reference material. The NIV is translated from older manuscripts, had a much larger translation team, and is in modern language. The KJV has much more reference material written over hundreds of years.

- The New American Standard Bible (NASB) is probably the closest trans-literal version into English, but it can be a little hard to read (this is a great version for studies of specific words).
- The New Living Translation (NLT), Good News Translation (GNT), and the Easy to Read Version (ERV) use simple language and help many readers to retain more, but are not considered to be the versions of choice for scholarly work.

Authors' note: We know of many that like to read various versions just to see the differing nuances. Many preachers use only one version, whereas many others preach using several. Again, it comes down to preferences.

Yes, there are some 'bad' translations out there, but they are typically not used in most evangelical churches. For example, the New World Translation has very simple translation mistakes in John chapter 1. Since this is a critical chapter in teaching about Jesus, this version should be completely avoided.

Likewise, only the Bible is 'God breathed scripture.' (2 Timothy 3:16). For both authors, if we had only one book in our lives, this is the only book (assuming a good translation) we would want.

'How the Bible Was Formed' Answer Key:
- Teaching, rebuking, correcting, training in righteousness, thoroughly equipping us for every good work
- It is from God and in those that believe
- The Holy Spirit

# WHAT IS GOD LIKE?

Many people think of God as 'the man upstairs' or 'the guy that went bowling and got the ball rolling.' Others may not think there is a God at all. And still to others, 'He's the guy that has long white hair and throws lightning bolts at our fun.'

But the Bible paints a different picture. God is unchanging and true. He loves us so much that He paid the ultimate sacrifice for us. Yet we live in a world of pain; and for many, they cannot see past that. You could be one of those people.

Most people form their ideas about God based on their experiences instead of looking in the Bible. They add to their beliefs by what they see on TV, the internet, or movies.

There are a few basic teachings about God that can provide a firm foundation in anyone's collection of beliefs. In later chapters, we will learn about the impact of bad choices (sin) and about the required sacrifice. But first, we will start our study looking at who God is and what He is like.

When we investigate who God is, we consider what kind of a God He is. So, we refer to this as the 'attributes of his nature.' There are several attributes, but this chapter will consider ten of them.

We will start with the first three, as they are strongly related. Bible college students learn very early that there are three 'omni-' words that used to describe God:
1. God is omnipresent (present everywhere). Take a look at Proverbs 15:3.
    a. Where are God's eyes? _____
2. God is omniscient (unlimited knowledge). Check out Psalm 147:5.
    a. Is there any limit to God's knowledge? _____
3. God is omnipotent (all powerful). Read the first part of Genesis 18:14 and Job 42:2.
    a. Is there anything too hard? _____

Let's consider seven more attributes:
4. God is holy. Flip forward to one of the little books at the end of the Old Testament, Habakkuk, chapter 1:13.
    a. God is too _____ to look upon evil.
    b. In the last book of the Bible, Revelation, chapter 4 verse 8 says, "Holy, holy, holy is the Lord God Almighty…" (mentioning three times is for emphasis – this is like saying in English, 'very very holy.'). Why is it important for God to be very very holy?
    _____
    _____

5. God is righteous. Turn to Psalm 116:5.
    a. List a few things in your life that could use some compassion:
    _____
    _____

6. God is immutable (His nature does not change). This is an easy one to remember. Look up Malachi 3:6.
    a. Write out the first sentence of this verse: _____

7. God is sovereign (the King of all). Turn to Psalm 29:10.
    a. Where does God sit? _____
8. God is merciful. Read Ephesians 2:4-5.
    a. God's _____ made Him rich in mercy.
9. God is just. For every sin, there is justice due. Look up Hebrews 10:30.
    a. If you have heard the term 'cause and effect' (every action triggers a reaction), this applies to God's justice. Our sin brings on judgement. But through God's mercy, if we accept the free gift of His salvation (discussed in greater detail in a forthcoming chapter), then this judgement penalty is paid by another (Jesus – this, too, is discussed in an upcoming lesson).
10. God is loving. Check out 1 John 4:7-21.
    a. God does not just love… HE IS love (verse 16). Why do you think there is a distinction? _____
    _____

Many people assume incorrectly that because God is a 'loving God' that nothing bad can happen. God created us with free will. We are born selfish. Our bad choices yield negative consequences. And this is compounded by all humans living in their consequences (good and bad). Good and bad consequences overlap with good and bad consequences of others.

God judges against sin. And to make this even more complicated, sometimes even nations can be cursed, even with God's followers living within them.

11. For many that cannot comprehend the choice to become a follower of Christ, like a young child who passes away from a deadly disease, there is great hope, as mentioned in Isaiah 57:1-2. Look that up.
    a. Why are they taken away? _____

God's attributes are important for us to learn and to understand. Nothing happens by mistake. God has a plan for everything… and He had foreknowledge of what will happen (this is one of the reasons why the Bible is full of prophecies).

Now that we have considered His nature, let's look deeper into who God is in the next two chapters.

'What is God Like?' Answer Key:
- Everywhere
- No
- No
- Pure
- (Personal)
- (Personal)
- I, the Lord, do not change
- Enthroned over the flood, as King forever
- Love
- (Personal)
- To be spared from evil

# WHO IS JESUS?

There is just something about Jesus. His name has affected millions. His name inspires love and it also hardens the hearts of the rebellious. For many His name brings joy. But for others His name is only spoken while swearing.

What is it about Jesus? Well, let's examine who He is. Several consider Him to be (just) a great teacher. Others prefer to call Him a prophet. Still others might call Him a philosopher that started His own religion. But the Bible is very clear who He is and what He is doing here (notice this is NOT past tense).

The Old Testament has several prophecies about the 'savior of the world' (the Messiah, or the Christ). In fact, 305 to be exact. For example, His birthplace (Micah 5:2, written 700 years before He was born) and even explicit details on His death (Psalm 22, written hundreds of years before the crucifixion method was developed) can be found.

But there is just something about Jesus.

Look up Philippians 2:9-11.
1. Eventually, what will EVERYONE do?

_____
_____

So, what did Jesus do to bring all of this upon Him? It started with our sin. Even due to our bad choices God still loves us enough to make a provision for forgiveness. (There is a following chapter on Salvation that adds more details to this.)

Jesus IS that provision.

In the Old Testament, God set up the 'sacrificial system'. This is where animals were killed and their blood was shed (drained out). This symbolized the 'spiritual death' that all of us are born with. Check out Romans 6:23 and compare it to Hebrews 9:22.

Jesus came to be the ULTIMATE sacrifice, "…once for all…"

Read 1 Peter 3:18.
2. Why did Jesus do what He did? _____

But to be the ultimate sacrifice, Jesus had to be special. John 3:16 tells us that Jesus is the "Son of God" (note the word "Son" is capitalized). There is only one Son.

This begins to reveal something very important in our learning journey. Here is a bigger picture: Jesus existed (with God the Father and the Holy Spirit in heaven) before He came to earth as a baby. In fact,

Jesus was VERY involved in activities that only God can do… our logical conclusion, then, is that Jesus is God.

This requires a little more explanation. The Bible reveals to us that there is one God (see Deuteronomy 6:4). Yet, there are three ways in which God works in our lives. The three are the Father, the Son, and the Holy Spirit.
- The Father (you may have heard the name 'Jehovah')
- The Son (this is Jesus)
- The Holy Spirit (God in spirit form that works in our lives).

You may have heard the term 'trinity.' If we break that word down, it refers to 'three in unity.' The Bible doesn't mention the word 'trinity' but it clearly teaches it.

There are times when God functions as all three at the same time (like during creation in Genesis 1:26, "Let US make man in OUR image…" (author emphasis). But usually we find where God functions separately, with the Father, the Son, and the Holy Spirit having separate duties.

Considering the Holy Spirit to be God is commonly undisputed (we will discuss this very soon in greater detail). But for many, understanding Jesus is God is hard to grasp. Clearly, Jesus existed with the Father in heaven before He came to earth as a baby, and then later rose from the dead… this may be hard to comprehend. But, that is exactly what the Bible tells us.

Read John 1:1. The person who is the "Word" was there in the beginning (this is the point of eternity before the universe was made). But also notice the 'Word WAS God.' This is a major clue that Jesus is God.

Now, slide down to read John 1:14.
3. This SAME PERSON became flesh on earth. What can we see? _____
4. And this glory is 'of the _____ and _____.'

Matthew 1:23 says that Jesus is to be called "Immanuel – which means God with us." This is believed to be His role (job description) here on earth. Thus, born as a baby, God is physically with us.

Now let's look at the name Jehovah. In most English Bibles, the name Jehovah (this is a Hebrew word so it is only found in the original Old Testament language) is usually in all caps, so when you read the name Jehovah in the Old Testament, you will see it as "LORD." In the New Testament, originally written in Greek, the name of Jehovah is usually written as 'Lord God'. So, keep this in mind for this study and when you read those names in your Bible later.

Continuing, Jehovah is commonly listed as the "First and the Last" and also the "Alpha and Omega". Alpha and Omega are the first and last letters of the Greek alphabet. This also refers to God being there in the Beginning (before creation) and at the End (in heaven forever). So, as you read these, understand they are interchangeable in meaning.

There is a fascinating trail of verses to add weight to Jesus being God…
   5. Read Revelation 1:8. Who is speaking? _____
   6. Holding your place, flip back to Isaiah 44:6.
      a. Who is speaking? _____
      b. How many gods are there? _____
   7. Now flip back to Revelation 1:17-18.
      a. See the name "First and the Last," who is speaking? _____

Since we know that Jesus died (on the cross to pay the penalty for our sin – also discussed in an upcoming chapter), and that only 'Jehovah is the First and the Last', then we have no choice but to conclude in these verses that God died on the cross. Our conclusion, therefore, is that Jesus is God (or as some may say, 'part of the God-head').

There are so many more verses that support Jesus as being God on earth. Let's consider a few more: We'll start with Colossians 2:9-10. Look this up.
   8. The term 'Deity' refers to God-ness. How much authority is given to Jesus? _____

Here are a few more questions to add to your learning about Jesus:
   9. Read Exodus 3:13-14.
      a. Who was sent to the Israelites? _____
      b. Now read John 8:58. Who is Jesus calling Himself? _____
   10. Check out Hebrews 1:3.
       a. What characteristic do both the Father and Son have?
       _____

   11. If we remember that Jesus is the Word (from the beginning of this chapter), many believe that (because of this name/title) Jesus is the mouthpiece of God. In reviewing the creation account of Genesis chapter 1, read also Colossians 1:15-17.
       a. Who spoke the words at the point of creation? _____
   12. Who do you say Jesus is? _____
   13. Why should this change my life?
       _____
       _____
       _____

'Who is Jesus?' Answer Key:
- Every knee will bow and every tongue confess
- To bring us to God
- His glory
- Son
- The Father
- The Lord God
- The Lord
- One
- Jesus
- All
- I Am
- I Am
- The radiance of glory
- Jesus
- (Personal)
- (Personal)

# IT OR HE? THE HOLY SPIRIT

Most people think of a person as a being of flesh and blood. But this is not the case with the Holy Spirit. However, there are things He can do that are person-like, making Him very real:
- He can speak to us. See Revelation 2:17
- He makes intercession for us (intervenes on our behalf). See Romans 8:27
- He dwells with us. See John 14:16-17.

Considering these, the Holy Spirit is without a doubt, part of the trinity. In the Old Testament, many of God's actions are noted as being through the Father. During the time of Jesus on earth, most of God's actions were through Jesus. But after the ascension of Jesus into heaven (after His resurrection), the Holy Spirit is sent to the Apostles (the 11 remaining original followers of Jesus)… and shortly thereafter, to all followers of Christ.

This chapter discusses what the Holy Spirit does.

The first time the Holy Spirit is mentioned after the birth of Jesus is found in Matthew 3:16-17.

The Father spoke from heaven while Jesus was being baptized. Then the "Spirit of God" descended upon Jesus. And near the end of Jesus' time on earth, we are instructed to "…baptize in the name of the Father, the Son, and the Holy Spirit." (Matthew 28:19)

One of the most conservative teachers of the Bible was D.L. Moody. In his book, Secret Power (Moody, 1987), originally published in 1881, Moody discusses key points for understanding the two primary actions of the Holy Spirit.

The Holy Spirit dwells inside the hearts of all Christ-followers. This is found in several verses.
1. Read 1 Corinthians 6:19. Paul is writing this letter to those that attend church in Corinth.
    a. Where does the Holy Spirit live? _____
2. Read Ezekiel 36:26-27.
    a. Whose Spirit is living within us? _____
3. Check out Ephesians 1:13-14.
    a. At what point does the Holy Spirit begin to live in our hearts? _____
4. Look up Romans 8:11.
    a. This same Spirit that lives in you is the same Spirit that _____ Jesus from the dead.

The Holy Spirit gives us power to serve God. This is a separate function from the above. The 'dwelling' is 'in' our hearts. But when it comes to serving God, the Holy Spirit comes 'on' (or 'upon') us to give us power. (Moody, 1987) (pages 60-61) Likewise, there are several verses that note this empowerment.
5. Flip back to Isaiah 44:3. The promise of God pouring His Spirit "on" is foretold.

      a. What happens to their descendants? _____
6. Look up John 20:22.
      a. What did Jesus do? He _____ "on" them.
7. Read Acts 1:8.
      a. What is received when the Holy Spirit came on them? _____
8. Slide over to Acts 2:3-4. Notice that the tongues of fire came to rest 'on' them. Then immediately after that, they had power to express the gift of speaking in other languages (that are not their own, as the Spirit enabled them) to preach to the Jews and to the foreigners in town…
      a. Take a moment and imagine what you could do to serve God if you had this power. Write down some thoughts:
      _____
      _____

Jesus told the disciples to wait until after His ascension back to heaven for the Holy Spirit to come upon them in Acts 1:4-5. But in verse 8, He clearly explains why: power to witness.

9. Write out verse Acts 1:8.
      a. _____
      _____
      _____
      _____

The combination of the indwelling and the empowerment (giving us power) for service are some of the most compelling aspects of our faith walk.

Go back and read verse 5. Notice that Jesus said, "you will be baptized with the Holy Spirit." For many of us, we understand baptism to be with water, either sprinkling or being dunked. There are a couple forms of baptism discussed in the Bible. To ensure we understand the difference, let's consider the history of baptism.

The English word 'baptize' has interesting origins. The earliest versions of baptizing came in the form of 'water-based public washing.' It got its start in (mostly) illiterate cultures where slavery ownership was publicly transferred (like in a town square) by the new owner performing ceremonial washing to show the transfer from the old owner. (Illiterate societies rarely had written contracts.) In most cases, the word means to immerse, but could be loosely translated as a thorough washing. For those that baptize using a sprinkling method, it is still 'ceremonial' but without the gallons required. For example, this practice became the norm in the Catholic church.[3]

---

[3] (Brom, 2004)

Fast-forward hundreds of years to the time of the printing press. In that era, biblical scholars began translating scriptures and printing them… but many denominations[4], Catholics included, sprinkled for baptism. So, instead of offending those that sprinkled, the translators converted the Greek word 'baptizo' to the English word 'baptize'. Since nearly everyone didn't know Greek, the method of baptizing (sprinkling or immersion) was left to the denomination. (Society, 2006)

One of the actions of the Holy Spirit is to give us special abilities to serve God better. These are called spiritual gifts. There are several. These normally work with each person's inherent personal skills. When a Christ-follower is serving God within their gifting, it is a special place. John 10:10 talks about having that 'fullness' of life. We will explore this concept more in the latter chapter about Gifting.

---

[4] A denomination is a group of believers that have similar beliefs and have organized into a group. Sometimes these are made up of many churches cooperating together. There is usually (but not always) an agreement for the local church to be governed in some manner by the overseeing organization.

'It or He? The Holy Spirit' Answer Key:
- In us
- God's
- When we first believe
- Raised
- Blessings
- Breathed
- Power
- (Personal)

# SALVATION

We all know we do things wrong. The Bible calls this 'sin'. We are all born sinners. This can be traced all the way back to Adam and Eve sinning in the Garden of Eden. And because of that, all humans are born sinners.

Take a look at these verses:
- Romans 5:12
- Genesis 6:5
- Genesis 8:21
- Psalm 51:5

For many of us, society doesn't teach this. It is as if we have lost our moral compass, throwing off our values from God's intentions.

God did not create us to robotically serve and worship Him. He created us with free will. Within this free will, we chose to do wrong (sin). With every choice, good or bad, there are consequences. The penalty for sin is death (yes, Adam and Eve could have lived forever if they remained sinless).

Romans 3:23 says, "…for all have sinned and fall short of the glory of God…" (NIV) 'All' means all of us. No one is sinless. Sin can be ANY failure in following God's law (see the 10 Commandments in Exodus chapter 20), or it can be any missed opportunity to do good, as noted in James 4:17. Not a single human, now or in the past, with the exception of Jesus on earth, has PERFECTLY followed this. We can't. It is not in our nature. We call this our 'sin nature.'

Based on this, we need salvation. But what for (or from)? The penalty is eternal death in hell. Romans 6:23 says, "When people sin, they earn what sin pays – death. But God gives His people a free gift – eternal life in Christ Jesus our Lord." (ERV) The 'death' in this verse is eternal death in the lake of fire (described as total darkness, completely alone, hot, and the 'weeping and gnashing of teeth').

But salvation is not just an 'eternal fire insurance policy,' there is so much more to it.

As we all know there are constant challenges we face in this life now, in John 10:10, Jesus states, "The thief's (the devil's) purpose is steal and kill and destroy. My purpose is to give them a rich and satisfying life." (NLT) In Christ, there is hope in this life, even in the midst of extreme trouble. James chapter 1 offers some additional insight on this. If you want, you can read that now.

Jesus, being God on earth, came with this message: a message of hope. In John's recalling of the time Jesus was on earth[5] in chapter 3 verse 3, "Jesus replied, "I tell you the truth, unless you are born again, you cannot see the Kingdom of God." " (NLT)

---

[5] Remember, there are 4 different versions of this – told by 4 different guys, targeting 4 different audiences… and nowadays we get to see them all, side by side in Matthew, Mark, Luke, and John.

There are two major thoughts in that verse. The Kingdom of God is heaven.[6] Being 'born again' is a little curious. You may have heard that term before, but it is easier to comprehend if you include the spiritual realm. When we are born, we are born physically… AND we are physically born with a dead spirit (again, you can blame this on Adam). When Jesus says you need to be 'born again', he is clearly NOT speaking of the physical.

In John chapter 3, he is talking to a guy named Nicodemus. Nicodemus asked for clarification on this and verse 5 spells it out. The 'water' birth is the physical birth (think of a womb's water breaking before birth). The 'spirit' birth is separate from this.

What does sin do? Well, it separates us from God. He is perfect and cannot be around sin. Thus, we are all separated from Him. But God loves us and does not want to be separated from us. He desires relationship with us. He made a way for us to be restored. This is through Jesus.
But, we have ONLY our time here on earth to decide. If we choose to become Christ-followers (for many, the term 'Christian' is overused to the point it has lost meaning, so this study uses the phrase Christ-follower), then we are forgiven and can be reunited with God (to a limited level while we are still alive, but fully in His presence when we get to heaven). If anyone chooses to NOT become a Christ-follower, then they are eternally condemned to hell.

Here are some study questions concerning Salvation:
1. Find Romans 3:23.
    a. How many of us are sinners? _____
    b. Therefore, how many of us are worthy of being in God's eternal presence? _____
2. Read Romans 6:23.
    a. What is the penalty? _____
    b. What kind of death are we talking about[7]? _____
    c. What is the gift? _____
    d. How (by whom, or in) is the gift delivered?
       _____

3. Go back a little to Romans 5:8.
    a. Romans 6:23 mentions that a penalty must be paid. But in Romans 5:8, who pays the penalty? _____
    b. Why does God do this?
       _____

    c. At what point does God love us?
       _____

---

[6] Most agree that God reigns in heaven, but because the Holy Spirit dwells inside Christ-followers, we know that this puts the Kingdom of God within us. Check out Luke 17:20-21 for more details.

[7] Check out Galatians 6:7-8, if you need to.

4. Check out 1 Corinthians 15:3.
   a. In the last part of this verse, we read exactly that Jesus "dies for our sins." What does this mean to you?
   _____
   _____

5. Find John 3:16.
   a. How does one accept this free gift from God?
   _____

6. Move to Romans 10:9-10.
   a. How, exactly, do we receive this gift from God?
   _____

7. Holding your place in Romans 10, read Acts 16:30-31. Then read Romans 10:9-10 again.
   a. Considering the definitions of 'believe' and 'confess' (check out the Glossary if you want to), what do these verses have to say about what we need to do to be saved?
   _____
   _____

8. The Bible gives no other way for us to be restored to God. Even before Jesus was on earth, In Genesis 15:6, we read about a guy named Abram (later to have his name changed to Abraham).
   a. What did Abram do to be right with God?
   _____

9. Can you see the simplicity of establishing our relationship with God? If you notice, NONE of these verses mention ANYTHING about 'being a good person to earn a ticket to heaven'. Read Titus 3:5-7.
   a. Why did God save us (verse 5)?
   _____

10. Many people confuse belief and faith. They wrongly use them interchangeably. Plus, it may help to think of Faith as a verb… an action word. Check out James 2:14-17.
    a. How is faith expressed?
    _____

11. Now read Ephesians 2:8-9. If we take into account the verses we've looked at so far, we believe God in our head/heart and we have a moment of salvation (see John 1:12, too). And our faith is walking with that belief to serve God… NOT because it earns our salvation, but BECAUSE of our salvation. Head to the Glossary and write down these definitions:
    a. Justice:
    _____
    _____
    _____

    b. Mercy:
    _____
    _____
    _____

    c. Grace:
    _____
    _____
    _____

    d. Faith:

_____

_____

_____

12. Read Romans 2:4.
    a. What does God's kindness lead us toward?

    _____

13. Look up Luke 15:10.
    a. What happens when someone decides to repent?

    _____

14. Check out John 14:6.
    a. How many ways are there to heaven?

    _____

Take a look again at question 11. Have you had a moment of salvation?... a time when you chose to cross the line of faith? If so, GREAT! If not, from this lesson you can see how simple it is. Confess, believe, and repent. This may be done in a prayer to God. Then, have faith to carry you through life.

If it helps refresh your memory, check out the chapter on Communicating with God to help you pray to confess, believe, and repent.

Obviously, there is so much more to the path, with many lessons to be learned along the way. So, continue with the next roadmap lesson as you navigate the path.

'Salvation' Answer Key:
- All of us
- None of us
- Death
- Eternal
- Eternal life
- Jesus Christ
- Jesus Christ
- Love
- While we were still sinners
- (Personal)
- Believes in Him
- Confess and believe
- (Personal)
- Believed
- Because of His mercy
- By our actions
- (From Glossary – question 11)
- Repentance
- Angels rejoice
- Just one

# FAITH

In the lesson about Salvation, we just started to talk about Faith. We learned that sin separates us from the love of God, and how God loves us so much He made a way to be restored to Him by having Faith in Jesus.

Coming to the realization that 'Jesus died on the cross (to pay OUR penalty) is what gives us the free gift of Salvation' can be hard to grasp; but when we do, it is exciting and burden-lifting. This can be quite hard for many to accept, as they cannot 'feel' this physically. We can't see or touch Jesus.

However, it is still up to us to receive this gift. (There may been a time when a gift was given to you, but you didn't want it so you didn't open it.)

When we accept God's gift, our relationship with Him starts. When we turn to Him, He wants us to trust Him and to believe all He tells us in the Bible. Faith is closely related to trust. In simplistic terms, Belief + Trust = Faith.

This trust is the cornerstone to our Faith. The book of Hebrews in the Bible, specifically in chapter 11, is considered by many to be the "Faith Hall of Fame." There, key players in the Old Testament, and how their beliefs drove them to act, are listed as examples we can follow. This list is full of NORMAL people. Every one of them is a sinner. And some of those sins are pretty severe. Murder, deceit, and sexual sins are common. Yet, God used every one of these people for His purpose.

And when we have Faith in God, we can trust Him with confidence. This fits the definition of Faith in Hebrews 11:1, "Now faith is being sure of what we hope for and certain of what we do not see." (NIV) Being sure and certain drives our confidence.

For several, it is hard to believe that God is that good. But the Bible is very clear about what kind of person God is. Hebrews 6:18-19 tell us that God cannot lie and that our hope in Him is an anchor.

The process is simple: God loves us. He is faithful. He keeps His promises. He promises us eternal life. We receive this gift by believing and having Faith. We live for God, having confidence in our salvation.

Here are some study questions concerning Faith:
1. Find 1 John 2:25.
    a. What does God promise us? _____
2. Look up Hebrews 10:23 and 2 Timothy 2:13.
    a. Since we know God is faithful to us, what happens when we choose to not have faith?
    _____

3. Consider Hebrews 11:6.
    a. Since we know that having faith pleases God, what happens to those that seek Him?
    _____

4. Take a look at Hebrews 13:8 and 1 Peter 1:24-25.
    a. With all of our emotions coming and going, what is one thing we can count on to be steady in our lives?
    _____

5. In Romans 10:17, it says "So faith comes from hearing, that is, hearing the Good News about Christ." (NLT)
    a. Where can you hear the Good News about Jesus?
    _____

6. Read John 6:37.
    a. Once we have faith and become His, what is one thing He will never do?
    _____

7. Romans 8:38-39 are classic verses. Check them out.
    a. Is there anything that can separate us? _____
8. Look up 1 John 4:7-8.
    a. Because God loves us, He commands us to love one another. List two or three people in your life who need to be loved.
    _____

9. Find Hebrews 12:6.
    a. This is a curious verse because many people assume God's love is always 'warm and fuzzy'. Let's look at this a little further…we know that a parent loves their child. But there are times when parents must discipline their kids. Parents love their kids enough, by nurturing and wanting them to be good – so they choose to discipline their kids. In the same way, God disciplines His children (followers) at times… because He loves us so much. Too many get stuck on thinking that God is a 'loving God' and that He wouldn't allow any negativity in the world – and so they reject Him because bad things happen throughout the world. (Check out Romans 8:28.) Can you think of a time when something seeming bad happened to you that turned out to be a good thing?
    _____
    _____
    _____

    b. If you think of Genesis chapter 3, who is responsible for the evil in this world (who lied to Eve that eventually led to Adam choosing to disobey God)?
    _____

10. Read 1 John 2:3-5.
    a. How can we be sure we belong to God?
    _____

11. Think back to John 3:16 and Romans 5:8.
    a. Even with all the evil in the world, how many of us does God want to spend eternity in hell?
    _____

12. The Bible commonly refers to God's people as sheep, as in John 10:27-29.
    a. How does a sheep know who the shepherd is? _____

Are you one of His? Have you heard His voice? If you have not taken this step yet, you can do so right now. Pray to confess your sins to God, ask Him to forgive you, and commit your life to serving Him. There is no sin too great that God cannot forgive it. Again, your salvation is not by doing good things, it is by trusting God. If you pray this, He WILL forgive you and call you one of His own!

'Faith' Answer Key:
- Eternal life
- He remains faithful
- He rewards those who seek Him
- The word of the Lord endures
- (Personal)
- Never drive away
- No
- (Personal)
- (Personal)
- The devil (in the form of the serpent)
- Obeying His word
- None
- They know his voice

# LIFE'S STRUGGLES

Life can be hard sometimes. And every now and then, it can be REALLY hard. One of the blessings of being a Christ-follower is that God will be right there with us, whatever the circumstances. One of the most important thoughts in this study is to understand that God is not the source of trouble. Trouble entered the world back in Genesis chapter 3 when Adam and Eve decided to sin by following the deceptions of the devil (in the form of the serpent).

1. Read James 1:2-4.
    a. What should our attitude be when trials come upon us?
    _____

For many, it is hard to think of having peace in times of hardship. Yet, that is exactly what Jesus promises.

2. Look up John 16:33.
    a. Think back to some troubles you've had, or are currently encountering. How does this verse make you feel?
    _____
    _____
    _____

3. James 4:8 has a great promise: "Come near to God and He will draw near to you…" (NIV) Find Psalm 46:1-3.
    a. For many, they find it difficult to find God in a time of trouble. They may even be mistaken in thinking God has left them. Since God promises to be 'right there' (as an "ever-present help"), what does '(you) coming near to God' look like in your life during a time of trouble?
    _____
    _____
    _____

4. Refer to Psalm 66:8-12.
    a. Since the trouble of this world is due to sin, God uses our consequences for His glory. These are called tests. Consider a silversmith who uses very hot fire to melt the metal specifically to remove impurities. List a way in which God has used trouble to remove one of your impurities:
    _____
    _____
    _____
    _____

5. Read 2 Corinthians 4:17-18, 1 Peter 1:6-7, and 1 Peter 4:12-13
    a. What are some of the results of trials?

    _____
    _____
    _____
    _____

Sometimes we bring the trials upon ourselves. This is the result of succumbing to temptation. There will be lots of times when we blow it, though. We are still human. Conversely, we have already established that God is Holy. And due to our sin, we are not. We all know that when we blow it, there are consequences.

6. Go ahead and review Romans 5:8.
    a. "…while we were still sinners, Christ _____ for us."

Temptation has its roots in the enemy of our souls, but now comes from our evil desires.

7. Read James 1:13-15.
    a. What happens when we give in to temptation?
    _____

But we can have power over our sin.

8. Look up 1 John 4:4.
    a. Describe a time when you were able to overcome a temptation:
    _____
    _____
    _____
    _____

    b. Who gives us that power? _____

The Bible repeatedly describes our relationship with God as like a father to his children. And, like any good father, he loves his children enough to discipline them to keep them on the right path of life.

9. Check out Hebrews 12:5-8.
    a. We are to endure _____ as discipline.
    b. What does that mean in your life?
    _____
    _____
    _____
    _____

    c. You can read more about that father/child relationship by reading through verse 13.
        i. In verse 11, what is the harvest of discipline?
        _____

On a happy note, God knows our limits. He won't put us in a situation we cannot handle.
   10. Read 1 Corinthians 10:13.
        a. God does not tempt us. So, who is tempting us? (Hint: Genesis chapter 3)
        _____

So, when we blow it, what shall we do then to be restored to God?
   11. Look up 1 John 1:9.
        a. Our path back to Him starts with _____.
        b. And when we do that, he promises to be _____ and welcome us back.

'Life's Struggles' Answer Key:
- Consider it joy
- (Personal)
- (Personal)
- (Personal)
- God's glory revealed, Christ's glory revealed
- Died
- We are giving it to our own desires
- (Personal)
- God
- Hardship
- (Personal)
- Righteousness and peace
- The devil
- Confession
- Faithful

# THE CHURCH

When it comes to the church, there seem to be a lot of questions. Why do we need to go to church at all? What does it mean to 'be' the church? What are the differences in denominations or beliefs? What does the church do?

Going back to about 1500 BC, God's people went to church in a tent (called the tabernacle), and then in a temple (built in Jerusalem) or in a synagogue (which could be found in just about any city or town). To some degree these are varying forms of churches. After Jesus ascended, the Holy Spirit came and entered the hearts of men and women. This changed the rules for church quite a bit.

1. Read 1 Corinthians 3:16-17 and 1 Corinthians 6:19.
    a. Our _____ is the temple of the Holy Spirit.

The Apostle Paul sheds more light on this in 1 Corinthians chapter 12.

2. Find verses 12:12-27.
    a. Paul refers to God's people as a body. If you think of this analogy a little further, he considers that Jesus returned to heaven (and so He doesn't have a physical presence on earth for now)... So, WE are His body on earth until He returns (details on that in a later chapter). Specifically looking at verse 13, we have _____ Spirit into _____ body.

So, what are we (the church) actually supposed to be doing? The answer is quite simple. If we keep in mind, from the verses above, that the church is NOT a building (but the people that collect as a group), we each have a role in what we are to be doing.

Before we look at what the church is supposed to be doing, let's look at what we, as individuals, are to be doing... we will then be able to see how this fits into our group (church) efforts.

3. Read Matthew 22:35-39
    a. The type of love mentioned here is the unconditional love that we would CHOOSE to have for another. In other words, this type of love is a choice; a decision to care. List the names of at least one or two persons you have chosen to care for:
    _____
    _____

Now let's take a look at a few verses that refer to what we (as a church) are to be doing:

4. Check out the first part of Matthew 28:19 (we will discuss the 2nd half of this verse in a moment). This is referred to as the Great Commission.
    a. "Therefore _____ and _____ disciples of all nations…"

b. Consider your answer from question 3a, how does 'going' and 'making disciples' affect this person (or persons)?

___

When it comes to the latter part of the Great Commission, we can see the physical act of baptizing ('immersing' in water, see the chapter on the Holy Spirit, above). Because of its location in the same sentence as the Great Commission, this stresses the importance of baptizing.[8]

There is another action that may also seem a little strange for today's society, the taking of communion. We find two accounts of this in the Bible.
Read Matthew 26:20-29 and 1 Corinthians 11:23-31.

5. In Matthew, Jesus is instructing His disciples by showing this example. In 1 Corinthians, Paul follows this example and provides additional teaching. Have you ever 'taken' communion? If so, what went through your mind the first time?

___

Additional thoughts on baptism and communion:
- These two things are considered the 'ordinances' of the church. You may hear this term, but it simply means things we are supposed to do.
- There is no mention in the Bible about a minimum age to partake in these two events. There are some cultural traditions that may affect this (like when a child is to be considered 'adult enough' to join in), but there is no specific age limit mentioned in the Bible.

As we think about the above, and we keep in mind that the church is any group of Christ-followers (and not a building), we are encouraged in Hebrews 10:25 to meet together.

6. Look up Hebrews 10:25.
   a. A church building is the most common form of meeting space. That is why many refer to the building as a church. But the fact remains, we are supposed to meet with each other. Why are we to meet? ___
   b. What might be a risk if we do not meet together?

___

In our society, many have bought in to the idea that we don't need to attend church; we can just 'believe'

___

[8] Notice that baptism is not mentioned as a condition of salvation… it is NOT required for salvation. It is a public proclamation of your faith.

and we are okay. We must remember that the church is not just a building or a place to gather, it is a group of people who are on a co-mission with Jesus. WE are the church. The building is simply a way to connect and be with other believers.

Think of it like this, if you are needing something, it's hard to do it on your own. The church, or group of other believers, work as a network when you are in need of help or resources. When you struggle is it easier to go it alone or with help? It is ALWAYS easier with help.

In the next chapter, we will discuss Spiritual Gifts. These are the special abilities God has given us, through the Holy Spirit, to do His work here on earth.

'The Church' Answer Key:
- Body
- One
- One
- (Personal)
- Go
- Make
- (Personal)
- (Personal)
- To encourage each other
- (Personal)

# SPIRITUAL GIFTS

We have mentioned above that the Holy Spirit grants us special abilities so we can serve God better. This is a critical part of our service to God. When it comes to serving God, we must never forget that we serve NOT FOR our salvation, but BECAUSE of our salvation.

Spiritual gifts are the supernatural abilities that God gives us. Spiritual gifts should not be confused with natural capabilities. Gifts are God-given extra skills and abilities that are beyond our natural abilities. They may be heightened versions of our natural skills, but they are clearly beyond what we have inherent inside us.

Note: The list of gifts recognized by any given church can vary depending on beliefs and definitions. For the sake of this study, we will consider 22, plainly listed in the verses we show. The authors of this study prefer to avoid saying when God will do His work (including handing out spiritual gifts), and when He won't, so we proceed with this study with the mindset that all gifts are available for today, but also that God will hand out these gifts when He decides.

The BEST part of being a Christ-follower is when you are living your life in the "sweet spot"; that intersection of your gifting, passions, education, and experience. When you are living in your sweet spot, you cannot wait to do your service. You are driven and loving it!

For many, serving God centers around the weekend service times, including doing things before, during, and after those services. For others, they prefer a 'behind the scenes' type of serving. And still others live every moment in their gifting (e.g. a missionary).

Let's consider each of the gifts.[9] Then we'll talk about some ways to discover your gifting right after the list.

Read 1 Corinthians 12:8. It mentions:
1. Wisdom
    a. This is a supernatural ability to understand the will of God.
    b. A young pastor once jokingly said, "Wisdom is the intelligence it takes to stay out of situations that require wisdom." (Rev. Mitch Klein, c. 1986)
2. Knowledge
    a. This is the special ability to understand spiritual matters. For many, this is in regards to biblical knowledge and being able to apply it in various situations.

1 Corinthians 12:9 continues with:
3. Faith
    a. Look up Hebrews 11:1.
    b. This gift is the total certainty of trusting God.
4. Healing
    a. The person with this gift usually prays for those with illnesses or ailments and they become miraculously healed. This is strongly related to Workers of Miracles (#5).

---

[9] (Rees, 2006), (Wagner, 1994)

1 Corinthians 12:10 we find listed:
- 5. Workers of Miracles
    - a. The person prays for powerful acts of God (usually beyond healing) that are supernatural, or so 'highly coincidental that they have to be miracles'.
- 6. Prophecy
    - a. Those gifted with Prophecy can communicate God's divine messages either in proclaiming God's truth or foretelling the future[10].
- 7. Distinguishing between spirits
    - a. This person has the supernatural ability to know when an action or words from another is from God, from human origin, or from the devil.
- 8. Tongues
    - a. For many, they recognize this gift to have two forms, 1) those with this special ability can speak to God (prayer) in a language that is not their own, and 2) those that publicly express a message from God in a language that is not their own.
- 9. Interpretation of tongues
    - a. This is the special ability to understand those that are speaking in tongues and to translate that message.

Look forward to more gifts found in 1 Corinthians 12:28. The new gifts found are:
- 10. Apostleship
    - a. Those with this gift have the God-given ability to oversee several churches.
- 11. Teaching
    - a. This is the supernatural ability to impart knowledge to others. This gift is commonly related to Knowledge.
- 12. Helps
    - a. Those with this gift help others to achieve their maximum ability (in their gifting) for God.
- 13. Administration
    - a. This special ability to plan and deploy effective plans for God-based organizations (churches and others).

Skip forward to 1 Peter 4:10. There we find:
- 14. Service
    - a. This gift is commonly found in churches, in a minister or deacon. It may best be described as one who serves another, but usually with the oversight of church leadership.

Look up Romans 12:6-8. In verse 8 we have listed:
- 15. Encouraging
    - a. Those with this gift have a supernatural ability to console or comfort another person or group.
- 16. Giving
    - a. This is the special ability to be exorbitantly generous. Those with this gift may or may not be rich, but they donate a large percentage of their income or goods, usually well beyond a tithe of 10%.

---

[10] There is a stern warning in the Old Testament if a prophet spoke of the future and was wrong... they were to be killed. See Deuteronomy 13:1-5.

17. Leadership
    a. This is the special ability to guide teams and to develop others to be leaders.
18. Mercy
    a. Those with this gift feel strong empathy for others and act to help them improve their circumstances.

Now find Ephesians 4:11. Here are a couple additional gifts noted:
19. Evangelist
    a. This person is gifted in sharing the salvation message (that 'salvation is in Christ') in a compelling manner.
20. Pastor
    a. This is the special gifting of a person to oversee the spiritual welfare of a group of believers (usually a church).

Read Ephesians 3:6. Paul discusses the grace (undeserved gift) to minister to the Gentiles (anyone that is not Jewish).
21. Missionary
    a. This is the special gift to be led to share the message of Jesus in other cultures.

Look up Exodus 31:1-6.
22. Craftsmanship
    a. This is the ability and knowledge to do all sorts of artistic work.


Authors' Note: Again, we do not intend to offend some by including or excluding certain gifts in this study. There exists a large quantity of varying beliefs and this list is designed to not be complicated or provoking.

Considering the list above, some may already be jumping out at you as gifts God may have already bestowed upon you. We have found a great link that offers some questions that may help you discover your gifting:
http://www.spiritualgiftstest.com/test/adult

Once you have completed the questions, you will be shown your results. Usually God blesses us with a few gifts… and these seem to fit the particular need at the time. And after the situation, the gifting may relax and we may not be able to express it in the same manner.

But one of the most important aspects of discovering your gifting is this: It should reveal what you are DRIVEN to do. This is what we will call 'living in your passions.' You are compelled and it may not make sense to others, but they don't have to 'get it'.

Write out your top five gifts:
_____
_____

Any surprises? _____

What are you passionate about that fits your gifting?

If money wasn't a concern, what would you be doing with your gifting?

We should mention some dangers with expressing your gifts… some gifts may 'freak people out', so be careful. It is unlikely God would want you to chase someone away from a chance at salvation or spiritual growth.

It is important to remember that no single gift is 'better' than another. Do not feel bad if God doesn't bestow a particular gift (or gifts) on you. He is perfect and your gifting perfectly fits you and God's purposes.

The key is to discover your gifting, put yourself in situations (e.g. volunteer) and use them. You will discover a huge amount of happiness and joy in your life. This is exactly what God intended in John 10:10.

Write out John 10:10:

'Spiritual Gifts' Answer Key:
- (Personal)
- (Personal)
- (Personal)
- (Personal)
- (John 10:10)

# LIVING FOR GOD

God wants you to live a life as close as possible to the example of Jesus. This is one of the major reasons why Jesus came. John 10:10 talks about having an abundant life.
1. Look that verse up.
    a. You can see there is a lot of pressure by the enemy of our souls. He wants us all to have a rotten life. But in Christ, we don't have to live like that. We can live a life to the _____.

The Apostle Paul discussed how we should live like him, but only in the context of him trying to live like Jesus.
2. Look up 1 Corinthians 11:1.
    a. What do you need to do to learn what the example of Christ is? _____

3. Read 1 Peter 1:15-16.
    a. What does being holy in all you do mean to you?
    _____
    _____
    _____
    _____

4. Find Psalm 119:11.
    a. What does memorizing scripture do? _____

5. Flip forward to verse 105.
    a. What does reading God's word (the Bible) provide?
    _____

The Holy Spirit guides us by helping us make better decisions. When we are in tune with God, we can know what the right choices are. In other words, we can do His will. How does this happen? We must continually fill our mind with godly things. For most, this means being a life-long student of the Bible.
6. Read Romans 12:2.
    a. For many people, they are spiritually similar to the generations before them, or the people they are surrounded by. This is the _____ of this world.
    b. When you do not conform, you will be able to test and approve (know FOR SURE) what God's _____ is.

We all know that sometimes it is hard to do the right thing. But sometimes we focus on the wrong things.
7. Check out James 4:17.
    a. What is the right thing to focus on? _____
    b. What is the wrong thing to focus on? _____
8. Turn to Philippians 4:13.
    a. Who strengthens us to do good? _____

Living a godly life starts at the point when we cross the line of faith. This is when the Holy Spirit begins His work inside us.

9. Read 2 Peter 1:5-8.
   a. What efforts might you take to ensure you have taken EVERY effort?
   _____
   _____

   b. In verse 5, what must happen BEFORE any of this can happen… we must have _____.

   c. Once we have faith, we can then try to do _____.
   d. Once we have goodness, we want to learn more by increasing our _____.
      i. How can you add to your knowledge of God?
      _____
      _____

   e. In verse 6, how does increasing your knowledge of God empower your self-control?
   _____
   _____

   f. Once you achieve a series of successes (in being self-controlled)… in doing so you are developing _____.

   g. In verse 7, having more godliness in your life opens up your heart so you can show what?
   _____

   h. When you show true brotherly kindness, you are truly showing your _____ for God and others.

   i. In verse 8, when you increase in these things, you can keep from being _____ and _____ in your knowledge of Jesus.
      i. Can you see why your knowledge is so important? Write out a few things that can keep you from increasing your knowledge of Jesus:
      _____
      _____
      _____
      _____

10. Find Galatians 5:16, and read 5:22-23. Notice this list is very similar to the one in 2 Peter, but reveals a little bit more of what is happening inside us. This list is commonly called the 'Fruit of the Spirit.' It is very important to note that this list is NOT 'fruits' (not plural). This entire list is one fruit. (It may help to think of each as a grape on a single cluster.)
    a. In verse 22, you can see the process begins when the _____ joins with our spirit.
    b. The next three, _____, _____, and _____, are more internal to what is going on in our minds.
    c. The next three, _____, _____, and _____, really come into play within our relationships.
    d. The last three, _____, _____, and _____, prove out in our walk with Christ.

11. Keep your finger in Galatians 5:22-23, but go back to James 4:17.
    a. When we focus on doing good, there is no _____ against it.

'Living for God' Answer Key:
- Full
- Follow His example
- (Personal)
- Helps us to not sin
- A light on my path
- Way
- Will
- Avoiding sin
- Doing good
- Jesus
- (Personal)
- Faith
- Goodness
- Knowledge
- (Personal)
- Perseverance
- Godliness
- Brotherly kindness
- Love
- Ineffective
- Unproductive
- (Personal)
- Holy Spirit
- Love
- Joy
- Peace
- Patience
- Kindness
- Goodness
- Faithfulness
- Gentleness
- Self-control
- Law

# BLESSED HOPE

"Life is pain, Highness. Anyone who says differently is selling something." (Reiner, 1987) This classic line from the comedy movie, The Princess Bride, is a tongue-in-cheek snapshot of our society. It is true, yet painfully funny.

In reality, there is a lot of pain in this life. As discussed above, Satan is the source of this pain. But God uses it to prove His love and to draw people to Him. There are some circumstances when God allows trials to be instruments of His discipline, too.
1. Read Proverbs 3:12.
    a. Why does God discipline us?
    _____

But, in the latter days, God will use catastrophic events to express His wrath.
2. Look up Matthew 24:1-35.
    a. In verses 6-7, you can see some of the most traumatic events possible. Yet, in verse 30, we see the Son of Man (another name for Jesus) coming back to earth to set up His kingdom. But check out verses 13.
        i. Anyone who stands firm will be _____.
    b. In verse 14, many versions use the word 'gospel.' Gospel means 'good news'. Re-write verse 14 using the phrase 'good news'.
    _____
    _____
    _____
    _____

Good news? What drives this? How can someone be happy in the midst of all the trials and tribulations?

It is because we have hope. Not just a hope of being happy today, or even tomorrow, but this is the kind of hope that we live our lives for… and the eventual hope of making it to heaven where there will be no more pain and we get to worship God forever.

If someone dies before Jesus comes back then they get to be in 'paradise' (just as Jesus told one of the thieves while He was hanging on the cross, as found in Luke 23:43). Paradise isn't the final heaven we will learn about, but it is in the presence of God while we await the End of the Age.

Let's take a moment to review a few events we've learned about:
- The Father, the Son (Jesus), and the Holy Spirit pre-existed before creation.
- Then creation happened.
- Then man sinned.
- Because of this, God set up the (animal) blood sacrifice system to 'pay' for sin. (This emphasizes the seriousness of sin. It is a capital offense that requires the shedding of blood.)

- Then God sent His Son (Jesus) as a baby to grow up (to be our example of godly living) and eventually be the ultimate sacrifice, paying a 'once for all' penalty.
- Jesus lived the life of perfection and became that sacrifice by dying on the cross.
- 3 days later, Jesus was resurrected from the dead and proved He had power over death.
- Jesus ascends to the heavenlies to begin to prepare a heavenly home for us.
- The power of Jesus' life, including His miracles, is the same power the Holy Spirit uses to indwell us (when we cross the line of faith) and fill us (regularly to empower us) to serve God.
- We live our lives for God.
    - If we die before Jesus comes back (to carry out God's wrath on the sinners that don't turn to Him), then we go to paradise.
    - If we are alive when Jesus comes back, then we don't have to experience a normal death.
    - Either way, we join Jesus when He returns.
- There is a final judgement at the end (more details below).
    - Those that are judged for their sin (those that are NOT Christ-followers) get thrown into the lake of fire.
    - Those that are judged by their good works (JUST the Christ-followers) go to the new heaven with Jesus.

Whew!

We want to take the remainder of this chapter (and the next three) to discuss the last few bullet points from the list.

There are a variety of views on the exact timing of when we will meet Jesus again or get to heaven. There are Bible verses that support one view and others that support a differing view. Because this is such a sensitive topic to many, we wanted to at least mention the differing views.

But we should start with the bottom line… if you are a Christ-follower, you have nothing ETERNAL to worry about. One day, sooner or later, you will be in the wonderful presence of Jesus in heaven.

But when the time comes, it will look like this:
3. Find 1 Thessalonians 4:16-17.
    a. Being 'caught up' is where we get our word 'rapture' (converted from the Greek word). Imagine what it would be like to be one of those. Write out some thoughts on that:

    _____
    _____
    _____
    _____

4. Let's break that down a little further. Check out 1 Corinthians 15:51-52.
    a. If we understand that 'those asleep' are the Christ-followers that have already died (from the time of Jesus until the time of this event); and that 'we will all be changed' refers to getting our perfected/imperishable bodies… so in the last half of verse 52, we get the chronological order in a nice recap:
        i. Trumpet sounds

ii. Dead rise and are given a perfect/imperishable body
iii. Those that hadn't died are caught up, too, and given perfect/imperishable bodies.
   b. See verse 53… this explains why we must have perfect/imperishable bodies… imperfect/perishable bodies cannot be in heaven.
   c. There is no mention in the Bible about our new bodies looking any different, but we do know that the few times heaven is discussed people are recognizable. So, you should be able to recognize other Christ-followers. Who do you want to see in heaven?

_____
_____
_____
_____

There are several ways to interpret (or explain) the verses that reveal the timing of the rapture event. But first we should mention a warning.

5. Look up Matthew 24:36.
   a. This verse clearly states that NO ONE knows the day or hour. Have you ever heard anyone 'pick a date' for the return of Jesus? _____
   b. Many have set a date, only to have that date come and go. Many good people have been led astray by teachers of lies.

But the ORDER of the events in the last days is what people have such differing views about. Here are the basics:
- Without going into too much detail for the sake of this study, we know that there is a 7-year period called the Tribulation (a time of great trouble, where God will begin His judgement of sinners by starting to pour out His wrath). And within that 7 years, the first 3 ½ will be 'good' years and the 2nd half will be very bad.
- The Battle of Armageddon will be at the end of the 7-year Tribulation.
- Then, there will be a period of 1000 years where Christ will reign on earth with His followers (more about this in just a little bit).
- Then the final judgements, with the Christ-followers going to the new heaven and everyone else, including Satan, getting thrown into the lake of fire… for all eternity.

Let's denote the three main differing beliefs on the timing of the rapture:
- Many Christ-followers believe that the rapture occurs at the very beginning of the 7-year Tribulation period. This view is called the Pre-Tribulational Rapture.
   o Considering the verses we have already looked at above, this viewpoint focuses on 1Thessalonians 5:9, which clearly states that "God did not appoint us to suffer wrath." (NIV)
   o Because the 2nd coming of Christ starts the last days 'clock', this means that Jesus could come back at any time.
- There are a few that believe that the rapture happens in the middle of the 7-year period, aptly named the Mid-Tribulational viewpoint.
   o This viewpoint considers the timing of the seventh trumpet sounding in Revelation 11:15, thus the 2nd coming would 'fit' into the events described in Revelation chapter 14.

- o Most scholars consider this to be the weakest stance of the three due to this viewpoint having limited support in other verses in the Bible.
- There are several that believe that the rapture happens at the end of the 7-year Tribulation. This opinion is called the Post-Tribulational Rapture. This viewpoint holds that Christ-followers are alive during the 7-year period and must endure all the wrath (targeted for those that are NOT Christ-followers) that is going on around them.
  - o Reviewing Matthew 24:29-30, this viewpoint holds that verse 29 is highlighting the end of the 7-year Tribulation… and THEN (in verse 30) Jesus appears in the sky (His coming).

There are two additional viewpoints that are somewhat related to the timing of the 'rapture and the tribulation'. Here are their basic definitions in the event you'd like to have further study:
- Post-Millennial – This viewpoint holds to the 1000-year reign, but there is no rapture before… and that we immediately step into the time of the final judgement.
- Amillennial – This viewpoint considers the 1000-year reign as symbolic (not a literal earthly reign of 1000 years) and, like the post-millennial position, there is no rapture and we step immediately into the last judgment.

Important authors' comment: Please note that some people are VERY passionate about the viewpoint they have chosen to hold to. There is a risk of being over-passionate and this can cause division in a church family. For most, this comes down to personal choice. We, the authors, certainly hope for the Pre-Tribulational rapture.

Division is clearly condemned in the Bible.
6. Read Titus 3:9.
   a. The root of the division is _____.
7. Look up 1 Corinthians 1:10.
   a. When divisions are eliminated, we can be united in _____ and _____.

Additional authors' note: Some religious groups hold to the belief when we die, we may be reincarnated into another body, possibly even an animal or insect. Others believe we have a waiting period (after we die so some semblance of penalty can be paid) before we can join Christ in heaven. Some even go as far as to say we are living in the afterlife and we need to make the best of what we have in our present time. Hebrews 9:27 clearly states that we face judgement right after death.

The Apostle Paul has a great teaching on this.
8. Read 2 Corinthians 5:8
   a. Any time we are away from the body (dead) we are in the _____ of the Lord. Given this, it would be impossible to be offered another opportunity at an earthly life, nor is there any possibility of a lag between death and being in the presence of Jesus.

Depending on your position on the timing of the rapture of the church, you will likely categorize yourself in one of the three common Tribulation camps. Considering all of the above studies so far, our

focus is to be:
9. Revisit Matthew 28:19.
    a. What are we supposed to be doing? _____

10. Revisit James 4:17.
    a. What are we supposed to be doing? _____

'Blessed Hope' Answer Key:
- Because He loves us
- Saved
- (Matthew 24:14)
- (Personal)
- (Personal)
- (Personal)
- Controversies
- Mind
- Thought
- Presence
- Making Disciples
- Good

# MILLENNIAL REIGN

Ok, with the previous chapter behind us, let's move forward in the chronology of the end times… to the time of the 1000 Year Reign. (The authors do not hold to the Amillennial viewpoint.) This is commonly called the Millennial Reign, too. Either way, it's still 1000 years. There is no question that there will be a 1000-year reign of Jesus on this earth AFTER the 7-year tribulation period (the 1000 years is listed right before the final judgment in Rev 20:6, so the 7-year tribulation must occur before). We will go over that shortly.

Regardless of your chosen position on the timing of the rapture, we all know that when it happens it will be very quick.
1. Find Matthew 24:27.
    a. How fast will the 2nd coming of Jesus be?
    _____

For many, they say that Jesus is already here or that the event will be small and insignificant. But that is just not true.
2. Look forward to verse 30.
    a. What will "all" nations do?
    _____
    b. EVERYONE that is alive will see this event.
3. Now look up Revelation 1:7.
    a. "_____ eye will see him…" and "…_____ the peoples of the earth will mourn…"

To begin the 1000 years, we are informed of a time when Satan is bound and cannot do his vicious acts on the earth for the 1000-year period. Jesus then reigns without the distraction of Satan on the hearts of men and women.
4. This is mentioned in Revelation 20:2.
    a. Satan is the _____ serpent… the same one that Adan and Eve faced in Genesis chapter 3.

At the end of the 1000 years, Satan will be released for a short time to do his nasty work.
5. Now check out Revelation 20:3.
    a. How long do you think 'short' is?
    _____
    b. The fact is, no one knows. It is not mentioned. But the lack of mentioning suggests the duration is not important.

You can see that the Bible gives specific lengths of some events. Therefore, we can map out how the end times will flow, but what we don't know is exactly when the clock starts. We looked at the verse that says "no one knows the day or the hour" (Matthew 24:36). Regardless, as every day progresses, we are one day closer to these events happening. However, there are some 'clues' found in the Bible to let us know when we are getting close.

A major event that tells us we are close to the end is a 'gathering' of the nation of Israel.
6. Read Ezekiel 37:21.
    a. We know that the Jews have been scattered across the earth, but in the final days, they are to be gathered back to the _____ of Israel.[11]
7. Find Zephaniah 3:19-20.
    a. God promises to _____ those that have been scattered.
    b. Can you imagine how God will 'deal' with those that oppressed Israel? What do you think that might be?
    _____
    _____

If it is ONLY the Israelites that get saved, how does this allow the non-Jews (also called Gentiles) to enter heaven?
8. Look up Romans 9:6, 10:3, and 11:26-27.
    a. In verse 11:26, who will be saved? _____
9. Read Romans 11:1-32.
    a. With the Israelites being 'branches' we can see, in verse 17, some have been broken off. The key is verse 19… the Gentiles are 'grafted in,' and therefore become part of the nation of Israel through the salvation efforts of Jesus. (Think of it as being adopted into the nation of Israel.)
    b. But in verses 22-24, we read that God may actually cut off 'dead' branches to make room for any Gentiles that become Christ-followers.
    c. In verse 17, the grafted in Gentiles are called 'wild olive shoots'. How does that make you feel?
    _____
    _____
    _____
    _____

Right before the very end (more details on that in the next lesson) there will be a time of great peace. This peace is nothing like the earth has seen, except prior to Adam and Eve sinning.
10. Flip back to Isaiah 11:6-9.
    a. We get a glimpse of this peace in these verses. Imagine your child playing next to a cobra.

We like to think we are all going to heaven, be with Jesus and our loved ones, and live happily ever after. Some believe we can obtain these things by simply being a good person or making good decisions. No one wants to evaluate what they are doing that could hinder their dream of seeing Jesus and family, but we need to. We need to be ready, we need to seek to not just do what is right, but rather what we are

---

[11] It is probably worth mentioning that many believe the 'clock' to the end times began ticking when Israel was re-given status as a nation on May 14, 1948, shortly after the end of World War Two. Since then, Jews from all over the world have been returning to the nation of Israel. (There is no way to prove this viewpoint, one way or another, but you should know this thinking exists.)

called to action.

Keeping your personal relationship with Jesus as your first priority, and loving everyone as Jesus has loved us.

All of the other things will take care of themselves. Our hope is in Jesus; we get to reign a thousand years with Him. And then spend eternity with Him. We are with Him as one.

11. Find Matthew 24:44.
    a. Write out that verse:
    _____
    _____
    _____
    _____

'Millennial Reign' Answer Key:
- Like a flash of lightning
- Mourn
- Every
- All
- Ancient
- (Personal)
- Land
- Gather
- (Personal)
- All Israel/all who call on the name of the Lord
- (Personal)
- (Matthew 24:44)

# FINAL JUDGEMENT

No matter what you think or what you have heard, a final judgment will happen. If you have progressed through this study you have learned there is no avoiding it (for those that are NOT Christ-followers); there is no hiding or running from it.

The chronology of the final judgement is simple. First we will look at those that are NOT Christ-followers:
1. Look up Revelation 19:19-20. Here the beast and the false prophet (these two are humans that play a major role at the end) are _____ into the fiery lake of burning sulfur.
2. Move forward to Revelation 20:10. Now the devil gets thrown into the lake of burning sulfur.
    a. For how long? _____
3. Continue reading verses 11-15.
    a. In the last steps of the final judgment, those who were not Christ-followers prior to their death will be raised and judged on their works. What happens if their names are not found in the book of life?
    _____

But did you notice something more about the condemned people?
4. Go back and check 19:20.
    a. What did these people do to seal their fate?
    _____
    _____

So, what is this mark? There is a lot of speculation and opinions about it. But first, let's read where it is mentioned in Revelation.
5. Read Revelation 13:16-18.
    a. The mark goes on the _____ or the _____.
    b. If a person does not have the mark, what happens?
    _____
        i. Does that mean they CANNOT buy food, fuel, or pay for housing? YES!!!!
    c. We see 666 listed, but who's number is it? _____
6. So why would anyone willfully take the mark?
    a. Go back to Revelation 19:20. Because of the false miraculous signs done by the beast, many were _____ into taking the mark.
    b. Flip back to Revelation 13:16. Others were _____ to take the mark.

What does the mark look like? No one knows. But it will be on a right hand or forehead. And without it, a person cannot buy or sell (at all). Going back to it being "man's number" (Revelation 13:17), many believe that the mark is a man-made marking or device. But no matter, ANYONE that has the mark has sealed their doom.

Now for those that ARE Christ-followers, the judgement will be very different. All Christ-followers will

have their name written in the 'book of life'.
7. Look at Revelation 20:11-15 again.
    a. "They were judged by what they _____."
8. Read 1 Corinthians 3:12-15 and review James 4:17.
    b. What should we be doing? _____

Authors' note: Our goal is not to frighten you into a relationship with Jesus, but to give you some insight as to why your relationship with God is so important. Jesus was sincere in his desire to reach everyone. The mission of the church is the same, yet we are to do as Jesus did to those in need.

We are called to love people. Remember, this kind of love is a choice to care. Do you see a need? Fill it if you can. Don't waste your efforts on those that are just taking advantage of you. Matthew chapter 24 is one of the best collection of verses on preparing for the end times.
9. But now read Matthew 25:31-46.
    a. What can you do to help the hungry? _____
    b. What can you do to help the thirsty? _____
    c. Have you invited a stranger in? _____
    d. Have you given clothes to the needy? _____
    e. Have you taken care of someone that is sick? _____
    f. Have you visited anyone in prison? _____

These are hard questions for many. But if we understand that these questions will be asked of us by Jesus at the end, then maybe we should do something now. Think of this as your final exam. Remember, we serve God NOT to earn our salvation, but BECAUSE of our salvation.

Here are some additional questions that may provoke some thinking:
- When my time on earth is finished, will I be able to stand before Jesus with confidence or will I be hoping to slide in before the gates close? _____
- What am I allowing to be part of my life that is causing me to sin or prevent me from doing good things? _____
- Am I willing to make the changes needed? _____
- Is there something I am doing that is causing others to fall short?
  _____
- What can I do to make sure I am not causing others to stumble?
  _____

When judgment comes to an end and all the evil has been thrown into the lake of fire, there is one more wonderful thing Jesus has in store for His followers… on to the next chapter.

'Final Judgement' Answer Key:
- Thrown
- Forever and ever
- Thrown into the lake of fire
- Received the mark of the beast
- Right hand
- Forehead
- They cannot buy or sell
- Man's
- Deceived
- Forced
- Had done
- Good
- (Personal – for the balance of this chapter)

# NEW HEAVEN AND A NEW EARTH

Not every religion believes in heaven or hell. Some just believe we live, we die, and we obtain a ticket to heaven when we have done enough good on earth. For millions, reincarnation is a staple in their religious views. And too many choose to believe nothing because it's all too confusing.

The Bible provides clear answers on how to get it right… in order to clean up this jumbled mess.

To review, Revelation 19 and 20 list the details of the final condemnation of those that deserve it. But the Bible gives us a small but wonderful glimpse as to what God has in store for His followers.

The Apostle Peter gives us one of our first hints that a new heaven and a new earth is coming.
1. Look up 2 Peter 3:13.
   a. The new heaven and the new earth are the _____ of righteousness.

In the final two chapters of Revelation John describes the new heaven and the new earth in striking detail.

A new Jerusalem comes down from the new heaven and sits on the new earth:
2. Find Revelation 21 2-4
   a. How does John refer to the new Jerusalem? As a _____
   b. Where is God's dwelling place? _____
   c. What has passed away? _____
3. Move forward to Revelation 21:10-27. Read it all, but focus on 21-27.
   a. What is used for asphalt? _____
   b. Why is there no temple? _____
   c. How is the city lit? _____
   d. Who gets to go inside?
   _____
   _____

At the very end of the book of Revelation, which is also at the very end of the Bible, John offers a stern warning.
4. Flip over to Revelation 22:18-19.
   a. What happens to those that add or takes away from the book of Revelation?
   _____

'New Heaven and a New Earth' Answer Key:
- Dwelling
- Holy city
- Among the people
- The old order of things
- Gold
- God and the Lamb (Jesus) are the temple
- The glory of God
- Only those whose names are found in the book of life
- They do not gain entry into heaven

# NOW WHAT?

After going through this journey using The Roadmap, what are your next steps? What do you need to do to make the changes in your own life, as well as help others make changes in their lives? All of us can improve… always. But are we willing? Be prepared to change, take the challenge to know Jesus more, and make Him known.

For most, the path to God is relatively basic:
- There is a point of time when God tugs at our heart and we listen to a message about salvation.
- Then we cross the line of faith (have a salvation experience).
- We begin to learn more about God… The Roadmap is just one of many tools that can help with this.
- (There is a step at this point that is commonly missed. EVERY Christ-follower is called to "…go and make disciples…" (see Question 1, below). This is NOT just for pastors and paid church staff. Once you have completed the Roadmap, we (the authors) urge you to mentor another through The Roadmap… and then they do the same after they complete it… and so on. In doing so, we continue to make disciples.)
- During this time (of going through The Roadmap and mentoring others after you finish) you attend church and begin to volunteer.
- (Our 'doing good' is not just limited to the church. We can and should do God's work all around us.)
- You may be compelled to volunteer more… maybe even a lot more… eventually working up to be a high-capacity volunteer.
- Beyond this, some may stretch themselves and go on a missions trip (and maybe go on one every year).
- And for a few, they may attend Bible college and seek to be in a staff (paid) role as a missionary or pastor.

Here is our mandate: Look up Matthew 28:19.
1. Write out this verse:
   _____
   _____
   _____
   _____

2. What can you do right now to start the process to make disciples?
   _____
   _____
   _____

3. List a few names of those that might be interested in joining you, as you mentor them, on The Roadmap?_____
   _____
   _____

Mentoring is not as complicated as it sounds. It may be as simple as having one-on-one conversations with another… both of you with your Roadmaps open… and a Bible for each, as you help them go through their Roadmap line by line. And, of course, helping them find another to mentor, too. And so on.

Your time mentoring may look like this:
- Start with prayer
- Read The Roadmap and look up every verse and answer every question
- Discuss and question/answer (e.g. 'What will I do now that I know this?'
- End in prayer

Authors' note: We strongly encourage you to read, study, pray, and journal. Prayer time is very important in your daily walk with God. As God leads you, you will be compelled to take action. For some, this may cause a radical change. If you are willing, God is also willing to guide you through it all. We dare you to pray the 'most dangerous prayer of all.' It's only three words… letting God know that you are willing to do His work:
- Whatever – are you willing to use your gifting in whatever He wants you to do?
- Wherever – are you willing to go wherever this requires?
- Whenever – are you trusting Him to take those steps at the time He sets?

We hope you have learned many thing about the Bible AND yourself. We pray for your growth and that you will have a fuller life as you serve God,


Authors,
Craig and Matt



For further study, we strongly recommend The One-Stop Bible Guide by Mike Beaumont. You can buy it on Amazon.com, searching for ISBN #978-0-7459-5193-5. You can read this cover-to-cover and it takes you through the Bible in a chronological manner that provides a wonderful historical perspective.

# APPENDIX A: GLOSSARY (OF COMMON CHURCH WORDS)

| | |
|---|---|
| Amen | What is commonly said to close out a prayer. It is translated "so be it" or "let it be so". |
| Baptism | To immerse someone in water to make a public profession of faith. This was originally done in ancient times to publicly show a change of ownership. |
| Believe | To make a choice to accept what the Bible teaches about Jesus. |
| Bulletin | The program you might receive when stepping into a church. These are usually helpful and full of information. |
| Charismatic | In context of church, see Pentecostal, below. |
| Communion | The practice of a group solemnly drinking a small amount of juice (or wine) and a small piece of unleavened (no yeast) bread or cracker to symbolize that Jesus' body was beaten (the bread or cracker) and that His blood came out to pay the penalty for our sin (the juice or wine). |
| Confess(ion) | Admitting your sins to others and/or to God. |
| Disciple | More than a student… a student that plans on making other students. |
| Divine | Of God. |
| Evangelical | A person that believes that salvation is ONLY through believing in Jesus. |
| Evangelize | Sharing the message of salvation in Jesus. |
| Faith | This is best translated as belief in action. Based on Hebrews 11:1, this is trusting God beyond our normal senses. |
| Forgiveness | The act of one not holding an offense against another. |
| Foyer | The lobby of a church building. |
| Gentiles | Anyone that is not Jewish. |
| Glory | God's full purity and beauty, usually glowing/shiny. |
| Gospel | Literally means 'good news'. |
| Gospels | The Books of Matthew, Mark, Luke, and John – 4 different accounts of the time Jesus spent on earth, written for 4 different audiences. |
| Grace | Literally means 'undeserved gift' (receiving what you do not deserve). |
| Great Commission | Our job description: To go and make disciples of all nations… |
| Intercede | Praying on someone else's behalf, or getting involved with. |
| Jews/Hebrews | God's chosen people. This goes all the way back to Abraham. |

| | |
|---|---|
| Journaling | A written account of your walk with God. |
| Justice | This is the assurance that God WILL deliver His wrath – the penalty for sins. |
| Mercy | NOT giving someone the punishment they deserve. |
| Ordinances | Within the church, these are the required (if at all possible) actions of baptism and communion. |
| Pentecostal | One who believes that all gifts are for today, including the speaking of tongues as evidence that the Holy Spirit has come 'upon' someone. |
| Prayer | Either out loud or silent communication to God. |
| Prophet | One who speaks for God, commonly telling the future. |
| Pulpit | The place where the preacher speaks from. |
| Rejoice | Being very happy. |
| Repentance | Being sorry AND turning away from your sin. |
| Sacraments | These are the sacred actions of baptism and communion. |
| Sacrifice | Taking on someone else's penalty, either willfully or not. |
| Sanctify/sanctification | The process of living a better life because of salvation in Jesus. |
| Sanctuary | This is usually a church's auditorium. Some are more casual than others. |
| Saved | The point in one's life when they have accepted God's gift of salvation in Jesus. |
| Savior | Jesus. The One who's actions save us. |
| Sovereign | A king or kingly position. |
| Tithe/Offering | A tithe is 10% of your wages. An offering is going beyond that amount. |
| Tongues | The spiritual gift of speaking in other or indiscernible languages. |
| Translations | These are versions translated from other languages. |
| Trinity | God, as expressed in the Father, the Son (Jesus), and the Holy Spirit. |
| Versions | NIV = New International Version, NASB = New American Standard Bible, NLT = New Living Translation, KJV = King James Version, (there are many others). |
| Witness | Someone who tells what they have experienced. |
| Worship | Worship can be just about any action we do for God, but is commonly referred to as the time of singing before (in front of) God. |

# APPENDIX B: SUGGESTED MEMORY VERSES

Psalm 119:11
Proverbs 3:5-6
Jeremiah 29:11
John 3:16
Acts 1:8
Acts 2:42
Romans 3:23
Romans 5:8
Romans 6:23
Romans 8:28
Romans 8:38-39
Romans 10:9-10
1 Corinthians 10:13
Galatians 5:22-23
Ephesians 1:13-14
Ephesians 2:8-9
Ephesians 6:12
Philippians 4:13
1 Thessalonians 5:18
Hebrews 11:1
James 1:22
1 John 1:9

# BIBLIOGRAPHY

Brom, R. H. (2004, August 10). *Baptism: Immersion Only?* Retrieved December 29, 2016, from Catholic Answers: http://www.catholic.com/tracts/baptism-immersion-only

GotQuestions. (2002, NA NA). Retrieved December 14, 2016, from GotQuestions.org: https://gotquestions.org/canonicity-scriptural.html

Moody, D. L. (1987). *Secret Power.* Ventura, CA: Regal Books.

Rees, E. (2006). *S.H.A.P.E.* Grand Rapids, Mich: Zondervan.

Reiner, R. (Director). (1987). *The Princess Bride* [Motion Picture].

Society, N. E. (2006, March 4). *What Is the Primary Meaning of Baptism? Some Translational Difficulties*. Retrieved from Bible.org: https://bible.org/article/what-primary-meaning-baptism-some-translational-difficulties

Wagner, C. P. (1994). *Your Spiritual Gifts.* Ventura, CA: Regal.

# ABOUT THE AUTHORS

Craig Dockstader studied Ministry and Biblical studies at Berean School of the Bible (part of Global University) and obtained a Ministerial Credential with the Assemblies of God in 2006. Craig also has a background in law enforcement and conflict resolution.

Craig and his wife have volunteered for more than eighteen years in their local church in areas ranging from children's ministry to youth and adults.

Craig has a passion to help people find their gifts and place those gifts into action serving their church and communities, as well as a heart for pastoral support.

His hobbies include sports, playing guitar, science fiction films, comic books and Hot Wheels collecting.

You can personally contact Craig at craigdockstader@gmail.com.

Matt Simonis studied interpersonal communication at George Fox College (now University) and graduated in 1985 with a Bachelor of Arts in Communication Arts and Telecommunications. He received an MBA from Western Governors University in 2009. He holds professional certificates in business administration, purchasing, and quality.

He served as a bi-vocational Associate Pastor for 20 years, eventually stepping to full-time ministry in 2014.

He is also Adjunct Faculty at Trinity Western University (twu.ca), teaching Leadership courses.

His hobbies include writing books (check amazon.com for more offerings), riding his Vespa®, and biblical scientific study.

You can personally contact Matt at k9mat@hotmail.com.

Made in the USA
Monee, IL
21 April 2022